1979

Leave a Touch of Glory

"Great truths are portions of the soul of Man;
Great souls are portions of Eternity."

JAMES RUSSELL LOWELL

Leave a Touch of Glory

HELEN LOWRIE MARSHALL

Doubleday & Company, Inc., Garden City, New York
1976

Dedicated
to
My Family
and
All Friends Everywhere

ISBN: 0-385-12306-x
Library of Congress Catalog Card Number 76–6203
Copyright © 1976 by John Stanley Marshall
as Executor of the Estate
of Helen Lowrie Marshall
Printed in the United States of America
First Edition

Contents

Leave a Touch of Glory

Leave a Touch of Glory

Have you watched the sun descending
In a cloud-filled, stormy sky—
How it leaves a golden halo
As it bids the day goodby?

Here a touch of glory lingers
Like a blessing on the land—
A touch of golden glory
From a strong and unseen Hand.

There are those whose lives remind us
Of the sunset's warming glow.—
They leave a touch of glory
Lingering after when they go.

His Gifts

Into every soul is born
A spark of the Divine,
A measure of Eternity
Within your heart and mine.

A gift of Love to you and me,
A promise of His care—
This light of hope eternally
Alive and burning there.

Into every soul is given
God's Power of endless Love,
Steadfast Faith within the heart—
All gifts from Him above.

A Bit of Eternity

I saw a butterfly today
So bright, so beautiful, so gay;
Oh, how I wanted him to stay,
But he kissed a rose and flew away.

I knew a moment's bliss today;
Oh, how I wanted it to stay,
But time will harbor no delay,
So it touched my heart and slipped away.

Just the touch of a butterfly's kiss—
Just one glimpse of ecstatic bliss—
But for the rose and heart of me,
Both meant a bit of Eternity.

Simplicity of Prayer

Prayer is such a simple thing—
    God's chapel is our own—
Just slipping in to sit awhile
    In thought with God alone.

Just opening and entering
    The chapel of our heart,
To rest awhile and talk with God
    And be with Him apart.

To pause awhile in quietness
    Within His gentle Peace,
And know the comfort and the joy
    Of prayer's profound release.

No hard-bound rules, no laws surround
    It's time, or place, or way,
For prayer fits into any
    Little corner of the day.

And what a joy it is to know
    The comforting release
From life's small cares and worries
    In that quiet time of peace.

Prayer gives strength beyond ourselves
    So mighty is its power,
That it can lend a radiance
    To every waking hour.

A radiance blooms forth in life
    Like flowers from the sod,
For every single minute that
    We spend in prayer with God.

Yes, prayer is such a simple thing
    To meet our God each day,
That we may live secure, and know
    He guides us on our way.

Outreach of Prayer

A prayer is a way of lifting ourselves,
Of getting a higher look,
Of reaching our thoughts to wider views,
Like reading a broadening book.

Prayer is a way of opening doors
We never had seen before;
From self-centered thoughts to those
That bring the whole world in rapport.

Prayer is an exercise of the soul,
Extending, enlarging our sight
To see our own life becoming
A part of all love and all Light.

Prayer of Trust

Lord, let me not be guilty
       Of the arrogance to be
Anxious as to what tomorrow
       Has in store for me,
In vain conceit believing
       That I, and I alone,
Must find the hidden answers
       To that vast and dim unknown.

I will, instead, be trusting
       As a child; will put my hand
With simple, childlike faith in Thine,
       Not try to understand,
But trusting in Thy loving care
       I will enter each new day
In humble gratefulness to Thee
       For showing me the way.

Heaven on Earth

Heaven's not a fenced-off place
In some far distant sky,
Nor is Eternity consigned
To some sweet by-and-by.

Heaven lies in every
Ordinary, common day.
We make our own Eternal life
Each step along our way.

Eternal time is measured
By a common hourglass.
We glimpse a bit of Heaven
As hours and minutes pass.

We only need the eyes to see.
The heart to count its worth,
To make our own Eternity
A Heaven here on earth!

From God's Love

This love that joins today
 Your heart and mine
Can only be from God—
 A gift Divine.

It comes from God's own hand
 A heavenly prize,
This gift of love that shines
 In your dear eyes.

'Tis born of God's own love
 For you and me,
A gift that He bestows
 So tenderly.

Wedding Day

This love of ours can only come
    From God—a gift Divine.
This love that binds our hearts today
    Before His holy shrine.

The wonder and the joy of it,
    This precious happiness—
The benediction of His hand
    Our union now to bless.

For this is born of God's own
    Tender love for you and me,
A bright reflection in our heart
    For all Eternity.

God grant we keep His gift of love
    Alive through all our days
To hold our hearts forever close,
    And close to Him always.

A Candle of Understanding

There is so much of darkness
    Encompassing about,
But deep within a candle waits
    To drive the darkness out.

The light of understanding
    Others' problems to perceive,
A gift that's freely given—
    Simply ask—you will receive.

A light of deeper insight
    Into problems others know—
A candlelight to guide us
    In the way that we should go.

To do our part to bring about
    A time of Peace on Earth—
A light of understanding
    Of our own and others' worth.

Rebuilding for Christ

Our Church now rebuilds for our Christ!
What joy and privilege it is
To work for the Master Builder—
To be trusted stewards of His
In building toward the future
With widening service and care,
His house in the heart of the city
His temple of learning and prayer.

Our Church now rebuilds for our Christ!
From the arson and fire-charred beams
Our eyes have been given visions;
Our hearts have been given great dreams;
From the ashes of hate and the rubble
He has given us faith to know
That out of yesterday's trouble
A better tomorrow will grow.

Our Church now rebuilds for our Christ!
Co-creators of His are we,
That God's Truth will rise from the ashes
And beauty from adversity.
Sharing this work of His Kingdom,
Attesting our faith and our love,
We build to honor and glory
Of our Master and Builder above.

The Crossroads

You met me at the crossroads,
Took my hand and led me on;
You met me at the crossroads
When faith was nearly gone.
When my confused and saddened mind
Reluctant, sought to stay,
Afraid to turn to left or right,
You pointed out the way.

You met me at the crossroads.
Your friendship, warm and true
Shone forth to light the way that led
To life and hope anew;
With gentle, understanding heart
You opened up the way
That I might find my own true self
In service and in play.

You met me at the crossroads,
Your life on mine took hold;
Through you I found new beauties there
And happiness untold.
You met me at the crossroads
I followed where you trod
Until I found my faith once more,
And through you, too, found God.

An Artist's Prayer

Dear God and Ruler of all time,
We, who roam the realm of rhyme,
The world of word and song and art,
Would seek Thy presence in our heart.

Give us the power to open eyes
To beauty of the earth and skies;
To open ears that they might hear
The angel voices ringing clear.

Lay Thy hand on our pen and brush
That we may, in life's busy rush,
Create a spiritual rest
That men may feel refreshed and blest.

We thank Thee for these gifts of Thine,
For every talent is Divine.
Then give us wisdom, Lord, we pray,
And guide us all in Thine own way.

Crystal Moments

Crystal moments—yours and mine,
Each one framed with light Divine.
Rare and precious, diamond clear—
Lasting memories to cheer.

Catch them; hold them carefully—
Guard them; keep them prayerfully—
Moments when the world stands still
High atop life's highest hill.

Heaven's very gates ajar;
You reach out and touch a star;
Moments crystallize to give
Beauty to these lives we live.

Greater wealth we'll never own—
Crystal moments we have known.

Man Above the Mountains

A mountain towering to the skies
Can trim a proud man down to size,
Can put a proud soul in its place
Can humble the whole human race—
Unless man looks upon the sight
With eyes to see God in its height,
With heart to understand that man
Is yet the greatest in God's plan,
That, crowned with glory, men of worth
Still stand above all on this earth.
Mountains crumble, cease to be,
But man lives on eternally.
Children of God—what greater grace
Need we to show us our true place?

Friends with God

He never speaks with loud and raucous shout,
Nor prays with frenzied pleas for saving grace;
In fact, quite often things he talks about
Are apt to spread a smile around the place.

He doesn't preach a fearsome God above,
Nor dwell at length on brimstone down below;
He, rather, talks about a God of love—
A Friend of his, he'd like us all to know.

He never wears a sanctimonious air,
Nor dons staid piety as one apart;
He simply has a message he must share—
And every word, you know, comes from his heart.

With dignity and zest he goes his way,
The selfsame way the Master trod;
And no one has to hear him preach and pray
To know he's one who's truly friends with God.

This Is the Road

This is the road the Master took,
Rugged and rough and worn,
The road that led to Calvary
Through shouts of hate and scorn.

This is the road the Christians took,
Rock-strewn and deep with mire,
The road that led to lions' den
And death upon the pyre.

This is the road the pilgrims took,
Beset by endless fears,
The road that led to liberty
Of worship down the years.

This is the road we, too, must take
If we would go His way,
A road made free for you and me
Who follow it today.

And may we never underrate
Those pioneers who trod
This selfsame road that beckons us
To climb the hills to God.

Timberland Stillness

Have you known the awesome stillness
Of the mountain timberland,
As if the world were silenced
By some word of High Command?

No birdcalls break the quiet;
All is right, is peace and good;
In this land of God's high country—
The stillness of the wood.

Make It Radiant

Make it radiant—this day—
Let your light shine all the way;
Let your heart run out to meet
Every creature on the street.
Take the whole world by the hand—
Let him know you understand.

Give a lift to one who's down;
Let your warm smile melt a frown.
Put the springtime in your stride—
Laugh with those you walk beside.
Scatter sunshine all the way—
Make it radiant—this day!

Meadow Lark

Was there ever a sound more brimming with cheer
Than a meadow lark's call in the spring of the year?
"Good morning, World, it's a beautiful day!"
The lilt of his sunny bright song seems to say.
"There's one yellow crocus, a purple one too;
With Spring in the air, the whole world is new!"
Glory and praise to the Giver of all,
Wells up in the heart of the meadow lark's call.

Memory

Isn't memory wonderful, though?
People and places we all used to know,
Lost in the mist of the passing of years;
Then a familiar face reappears,
And suddenly there it all happens again
As clearly in your mind as it was then.

The happy, the sad, the good and the bad—
Every experience you have ever had
Filed neatly away—how can it be—
This awsome computor called memory?
If anyone doubts the Divine in Man,
Let him explain memory if he can.

A Gardener Sees

Oh, a gardener's eyes are magic eyes
That see what cannot be seen,
That look on plots of dry, parched earth
And see them fresh and green.

Through his magic eyes a gardener
Can see in a small, brown pod
A bit of Heaven lying there,
For a gardener works with God.

Oh, a gardener's eyes are happy eyes
In tune with the sun and shower,
And tomorrow's joys are his today
In his magic world of flowers.

Mountain Beauty

The air is crisp and fresh and clean,
    The sky as blue as the sea,
A few white clouds, like ships at sail
    Ride on majestically.

The aspens quivering ecstasy,
    And every stalwart pine
Whisper their joy at being alive
    On a day so wondrous fine.

Here hummingbirds dart playfully
    Or hover joyously,
And I'm part of this lovely world,
    And it is part of me!

A Lovely Time to Walk

He who trod the country roads,
    Close to Nature's ways,
Must have loved the autumn with
    Its crisp and brilliant days.

He must have smiled to see the purple
    Daisy's perky face,
To hear the whispering leaves and sense
    The gently slowing pace.

He must have loved the sight of grain
    Grown golden on the stalk;
He must have found the autumn time
    A lovely time to walk.

West Wind Gossip

What's happening to the westward
To excite the pine trees so?
What gossip has sent them adancing
As the west winds sigh and blow?

Can't you sense the quivering tension?
How quiet but strained they are;
Then bow and nod to the west wind,
The bearer of news from afar.

It must be good news, and exciting,
For they sway with delight and start dancing.
Whatever is stirring the west wind
Tells Mother Nature's romancing.

Whatever the gossip the pine trees hear,
Whatever the west winds bring,
If it makes the pine trees dance for joy,
It makes my own heart sing.

A Heaven Below

Let there be goodness and beauty,
And let there be eyes to see
Hearts stilled to reverent quiet,
Knowing it all comes from Thee.

All hushed before the beauty
Of a sunset's glorious sky;
Let there be soft and gentle things—
A mother's sweet lullaby.

Let there be light and loveliness,
And let there be ears to hear
The sigh of wind in the branches,
The bird song ringing clear.

Let there be truth and honor,
And let there be minds that know
That beauty, goodness, light and love
Make life a Heaven below.

Secret Formula

Sometimes seeds sown in seasons
  Unremembered, past recall,
Grow and bear the finest fruits
  And flowers of them all.
A word we may unthinking, speak,
  May fall on fertile ground,
And far surpass in harvest all
  The other words around.

And since we never can be sure
  Which of the seeds we sow
Will hold the secret formula
  For causing good to grow,
About all we can really do
  Is make sure such a seed
Is tucked away in every daily
  Word and thought and deed.

A Pocket of Smiles

Each morning pack a pocket of smiles,
    Enough to last the day,
And scatter them with a lavish hand
    Along your daily way.

It's a curious thing, but the more you give
    The more your supply will grow,
And at set of sun when the day is done
    Your pockets will overflow!

Each morning pack a pocket of smiles,
    Enough to last the day,
And you'll leave a trail of happiness
    As long as life's whole way!

Enter Singing

Each morning a new play begins,
The stage is cleared of bygone sins,
Old hurts, old fears, all cleared away
To make room for this new Today.

Dawn's overture has reached its crest;
Anticipation stirs each breast
As starry curtain, slowly furled,
Enthralls a hushed and waiting world.

The scene is beautiful and bright,
Illumined by Hope's morning light,
Dew-fresh and sparkling clean and new,
As in the wings, we wait our cue.

The Master, who directs the play,
Speaks softly, "This is your Today;
On you depends the joy it's bringing—
Go forth now—and enter singing!"

New Mornings

New mornings—each a precious gift
    Alike to rich and poor,
Fresh with promise, bright with hope,
    Delivered at our door.

Tied with ribbons of the dawn
    To give the heart a lift,
Never two the same—each one
    A very special gift.

To be accepted graciously,
    As in the spirit given
By that Creator of all days;
    Delivered fresh from Heaven.

New mornings—new beginnings—
    Alike for rich and poor,
A never-failing gift of Hope
    Left daily at our door.

New Friend

There's a special little halo
That crowns the days that end
With the happy, warming knowledge
That you've made a brand-new friend.

Though you wouldn't take a fortune
For the old friends that are yours,
The making of a new friend
Always opens other doors.

Your world is wider, richer
With every new friend won,
With the hope of glad tomorrows
In a friendship just begun.

A special little halo
Gives that day a brighter hue,
And a very special halo
Crowns the day that I found you!

Have I, Today?

I look back on this day that is gone—
On the people I've met since its glorious dawn;
As their paths crossed with mine did the sun
    brighter shine;
Had they happier thoughts for the day to think on?

As the day wore on, by word or by letter,
Did I make someone feel just a bit better?
Could I have said something to help and inspire,
Someone to walk with his head a bit higher?

Perhaps I, with no more than a smile
Could shorten another's heartbreaking mile.
Did I really do something to make anguish smaller;
This day have I really helped someone walk taller?

Eyes of Understanding

Let me see life through a thousand eyes,
    The eyes of the young and old,
The tear-filled eyes and the laughing eyes,
    The eyes of the faint and bold.

Let me feel hurt as my neighbor feels,
    And thrill to his happiness;
Let me cringe at the blow the other one takes,
    Or glow with another's success.

Let me stand in the footsteps of every man
    Who travels on paths with me;
Let me understand him as only I can
    When I see what his own eyes see.

"I owe no man," he proudly said,
But his neighbor bowed his humble head;
"I'm every man's debtor," his voice was low,
"All that I have, to others I owe.
Right from the moment of my birth
My debts began to build on earth.

"For the love, the strength and faith I drew
From others—loved ones helped me too.
The little I've done toward success—
To them I owe my happiness.
To strangers sharing gifts with me,
People I shall never see.

"'Little people,' the world calls such—
I owe them all so very much.
To skills of work-worn hands—to these
I owe my pleasant life of ease.
The debts of gratitude I owe
I never can repay, I know.

"A debtor I shall always be—
I owe every man," said he.

I Am Not Blind

You say that I've gone blind and pity me—
But oh, there are so many do not see
The beauty God has placed at every turn
Though having eyes; 'tis they who need concern.

For I am wealthy, rich beyond compare,
For I have loyal friends who know and care;
I have the love of family and can see
The face of every one who's dear to me.

And oh, I'm very rich in memory,
Each sunset that I've seen belongs to me;
The summer breezes and the winter's snow,
The spring, the fragrance of a rose, I know.

I own the happiness that we have shared;
The knowledge my beloved has always cared;
The sky is mine; the freshness of the sod;
I have a special closeness now to God.

I've oh so many blessings, great and small.
I've only lost my outer sight, that's all.
My inner sight is clear as clear can be;
I am not blind, for now I truly see.

Research Scientist

This is the road I have chosen;
This is the road I must take
And follow it out to its ending
For my own and the whole world's sake.

For if I should find the answers,
The world would partake of my gain,
And if it should lead to nothing,
It still would not be in vain.

For others who follow after
In search of the truth will know
The road I have chosen is fruitless,
And seek other ways to go.

The world will be richer for sharing
The progress—and errors—I make.
This is the road I must follow;
This is the way I must take.

The Road to Success

The road to success has many a turn
    And many a sudden bend,
But, strangely enough, the road to success
    Is a road that has no end.

We may look ahead on our upward climb
    To a far-off, sun-crowned peak,
And we tell ourselves that it must surely be
    The goal—the success we seek.

But when we have labored that last hard mile,
    Gained what we thought was the crest,
Revealed is a new peak farther on—
    Here's only a place to rest.

No, the road to success is an endless one,
    And only a fool will say,
"At last I have come to the end of the road
    And success is mine today."

Life Meets You

Enter into the game of life;
Play it for all it's worth;
Gladly accept every day that comes
And live every minute on earth.

Enter into the joy of life;
Join eager hands in the fun;
Don't be content with a laggard soul;
Go into the races and run.

Enter into the zest of life—
The challenge of today's game;
Don't be a loser simply because
Your determination went lame.

Enter into the love of life—
The glory of each new day;
Go forth to meet life with a smile,
And life meets you more than halfway!

Fellowship

Fellowship's a maker of friendships—
Think back on your life and see
How many friendships you can trace
To this spirit of harmony.

Fellowship—working with others
Has a way of bringing to light
Talents and gifts we might never know
With only a greeting polite.

Fellowship's more than the privilege
Of getting to know each other;
It's a Christian obligation
To join hands with your brother.

It's a Christian's obligation
To share in work to be done,
And the good Lord adds fellowship
To make the work seem more fun.

Yes, fellowship is God's own way
Of joining with labor and mirth
The hands and hearts of His people
In building His kingdom on earth.

When You Dream

When you dream, may the dream be worthy
Of the best that in you lies;
Wide as the distant horizon,
High as the open skies.

Deep as the welling of strong desire,
Far as the farthest star;
May your dreams reveal beyond
Things better than they are.

Dreams—great dreams have the power to lift,
To alter the lives of men;
Dreams—the windows of the soul,
That can give man hope again.

Faith in Yourself

Does the task ahead seem much too hard;
Do you hesitate to get started?
Is it too much to ask, this difficult task;
Do you feel yourself weak and fainthearted?

This is the time to surprise yourself,
To show yourself what you can do;
You'll be amazed, if you only start
What powers are given you!

With the will to begin the task ahead,
And go as far as you can,
You'll surprise yourself what persistence will do,
And faith in yourself as a man!

May-Day

When I was small, I lived in a town
Flanked by a shady wood
With a friendly old creek that wound its way
All through my little-girlhood.

White and blue the violets grew,
Nestled there in the shade,
And Dutchman's-breeches, saucy pink,
Brightened the leaf-covered glade.

Every Jack-in-the-Pulpit was
A special treasure found,
And starlike, white Anemone
Smiled from the leaf-rich ground.

We'd load our small red wagon
Full with blossoms wild and sweet
To top our gay May-baskets
With their homemade candy treat.

I wonder if the woods still stand,
The old creek running through,
And if the children hunt wild flowers
The way we used to do.

I wonder if they ring doorbells,
Then scamper off and hide,
As small friends find the baskets
And take them all inside.

Memorial Day

Our fathers sacrificed so much
    To bring us liberty,
And many gave their lives that we
    Might be strong and free.

We think of family, home, and friends,
    This great land of the free
Where we can worship as we choose,
    Be what we want to be.

How glad we are to be alive
    In such a glorious day;
How grateful for the strength to meet
    Each challenge on our way!

This is the time we try to voice
    All that's in our heart,
And surely God must know and bless
    This day we set apart.

Love This Land

Love this Land—its mighty mountains
Pointing skyward, tall and grand;
Love its prairies, rolling prairies
Stretching far on every hand.

Love its rivers, lazy rivers,
Wooded lakes and mountain streams.
Love its people, handsome people,
Gentle people with their dreams.

Love its cities, teeming cities
Gleaming progress everywhere.
Love its small towns, quiet small towns,
Little home towns scattered there.

Love this Land, my native Land,
This beloved wonderland!
Love its freedom—precious freedom—
Our own right where free men stand.

Thanksgiving Day

This is the time, that special time,
The day we set apart
To try to voice the gratitude
We feel deep in our heart.

The time when we become aware
Of blessings, great and small,
And realize we never can
Give proper thanks to all.

But since God understands and hears
The language of the heart,
I'm sure He knows and cherishes
This day we set apart.

Hills Are for Climbing

Hills are for climbing; ask any small boy;
He'll vouch for the lure of a hill, and the joy
Of scrambling skyward with never a stop
Till, heady with triumph, he stands at the top.

Hills are for climbing, and dreary indeed
Would life be if were we never to heed
The challenge to conquer an unknown hill
Demanding our utmost in courage and skill.

The higher the hill, the broader the view;
The greater the challenge is, too.
Ask any small boy—he'll vouch for the thrill
Of standing triumphant there—King of the Hill!

The Star of Castle Rock

Long years ago in Bethlehem
A star shone brilliant bright
Above the place where Christ was born
On that first Christmas night.

And Wise Men, following its gleam,
Came traveling from afar
To see the miracle that lay
Beneath that glorious star.

Tonight we light our Christmas star
In memory of that birth,
Proclaiming to the world our wish
For peace, goodwill on earth.

A star whose radiant glow reveals
The close encircling ties
That bind the hearts of all whose hands
Have placed it in the skies.

A beacon light whose beams reach out
And lift the hearts of men,
That they may sense the wonder
Of His coming once again.

That travelers by earth and sky
Who journey through the night
May feel the warmth and peace and cheer
Reflected in its light.

For now, as then, the star proclaims
A miracle sublime—
The miracle of love reborn
Each blessed Christmastime.

And as the star of Bethlehem
Declared the Savior's birth,
May this, the Star of Castle Rock,
Shine forth for Peace on Earth.

EXPLANATORY NOTE: A forty-five-foot electric lighted star atop a massive, castlelike butte overlooks Castle Rock, a thriving town on Highway No. 25 south of Denver, Colorado. Each year the star is lighted for the Christmas season. The lighting ceremony features music, prayer, and speeches, and for several years the foregoing poem was recited by the author.

Another Year

I swear, the way time passes
Is a cotton-pickin' crime;
Still, I reckon there are some things
That jes' naturally take time.

Like, fer instance, in this past year
Seems we've come to love you more,
And we sorta feel we know you
Better than we did before.

Yessir, life sure does seem richer
For this year that's passed away,
So, let's say you've really earned it—
Have a great big happy day!

When Do We Eat?

My bride's in the kitchen
With flour-smudged nose,
Wearing her very best
Housewifely pose.

The cookbook lies open;
The kitchen's a mess;
What she's concocting
Is anyone's guess.

She's cooking dinner
That's fit for her king—
Provided that she can
Decipher the thing.

If not, and such is
The fate of beginners,
Thank the good Lord
There are still TV dinners!

Grandma's Gumption

Everyone has her down days
When everything seems to go wrong,
And your spirits sink in self-pity
As the drab hours drag along.

My grandmother's life was not easy,
And she had her dark days too,
But she had a sort of workable faith
That always carried her through.

"No use cryin' over spilt milk,"
  She'd say in her homely way,
"We've moped long enough; now it's time to work;
  Got my gumption back today."

I would recall how the sun came out,
And things weren't nearly so black
When Grandma rolled up her sleeves and we'd know
That she had her gumption back.

Baby Sister

What good's a baby sister
Anyway, I'd like to know.
So far as I can see, she's good
For nothin', 'cept for show.

All she does is sleep and sleep
And sleep some more, and then
Wake up and holler till she's fed
Then go to sleep again.

She's awful dumb—she can't play ball,
Or ride a bike, or swing,
Or climb a tree, or roller-skate—
She can't do anything.

To go and get a girl when then
They could have had their pick
Of boys or dogs or anything!—
It sure does make me sick.

But, since we're stuck with her, I guess,
(Doc says we can't return her)
I'll have to just make up my mind
I'm gonna have to learn her.

Results in Reverse

A fact which may seem strange to you,
With results in reverse—you'll see—
The more you love and the more you give,
The richer your own life will be!

For every selfless gift of love
And every real sacrifice
Will bring love back to you tenfold,
And will more than repay your price.

Loving never emptied the heart,
Nor giving the purse—that's true!
The more you give, the more you have,
And the more that comes back to you.

To God with Love

We've all known that special lift
Felt when we bestow a gift
On some dear one—a friend or kin.
Little card, "With love," tucked in.

There is no begrudging there—
Such a joy it is to share
Blessings that we have with others,
Friends and neighbors, sisters, brothers.

Such a happy way to say
That they're loved a special way;
Such a nice way to express
All our love and gratefulness.

So it is with gifts we bring
As our heart's thank-offering
Token of our gratitude
For the beautiful and good.

Symbol of our grateful praise
For His blessings all our days.
Thus, we give our Friend above
These, our gifts—"To God with love."

Beyond

Beyond the reach of reason,
Beyond the farthest star
The questing heart seeks out the truth
Farther and ever far.

The searching soul looks upward,
Higher and ever high
Where faith alone can sense the way
Above, beyond the sky.

Beyond the mind's horizons,
Beyond all time and space,
Man's deepest self will not be stayed
Until he sees God's face.

Symphony of Beauty

No lovelier time is there than set of sun
When glories of the day are held in one
Large symphony of beauty, flame of gold,
One breathless harmony for hearts to hold.

Just so, no lovelier time of life is there
Than when at eventide, serenely fair,
Life's golden setting sun in peace unfolds
The best of all that's past, its flame of gold.

The joy and golden worth of days gone by
Reflected in a loved one's evening sky,
She faces west, and makes life's sunset there
A flame of beauty with her gifts to share.

Arriving—Not Leaving

My dearest ones, don't grieve for me,
I'm arriving, I'm not leaving—
Another step in Eternity—
Cause for rejoicing, not grieving.

Another step upward, wherever that be,
And none of us are knowing;
But all a part of God's great plans,
And where?—we must leave to His showing.

Be glad for the happy times we've shared,
The love and the joys that were ours,
The bright sunny days with never a care,
The rainbows after the showers.

This is a natural thing I do,
This adventurous thing called Death,
But life does not end, nor the soul cease to be
By the stopping of heartbeat and breath.

Please—do not grieve. Try to believe
I am here, though you cannot see,
For in spirit I'm standing close beside,
And shall through Eternity.

A new book of inspirational verse by one of America's most popular poets. In this collection, Mrs. Marshall's poetry reveals and radiates a profound love of God, love of humanity, and love of nature. Such poems as "Leave a Touch of Glory," "Timberland Stillness," "Meadow Lark," and "A Gardener Sees," evoke a spirituality in man's relationship with nature that is a new element in Mrs. Marshall's work. Her treatment of these and other real and meaningful themes is unpretentious yet deeply touching, which is why so many thousands of readers have found comfort and joy in her words.